Fishlock's
Sea Stories

Also by Trevor Fishlock

Fishlock's Wildtracks
More Fishlock's Wildtracks

Fishlock's Sea Stories

Trevor Fishlock

seren

Seren is the book imprint of
Poetry Wales Press Ltd
Nolton Street, Bridgend, Wales
www.seren-books.com

First published 2003
© Trevor Fishlock, 2003

ISBN 1-85411-360-7
A CIP record for this title is available
from the British Library

The publisher works with the financial assistance
of the Welsh Books Council

Printed in Plantin by Gomer, Llandysul

This book is based on the BBC Wales television series
Fishlock's Sea Stories, written and presented by Trevor
Fishlock, directed by Phil Lewis and produced by Ceri
Wyn Richards. Series consultant Dr David Jenkins. The
programmes are a Torpedo production for BBC Wales.

Contents

Introduction

In the beginning was the ship

For as long as I can remember I have been drawn to the sea. I was brought up close to the shore, my early years framed by beaches and cobbled quays, the spectacle of ships and the rhythm of tides. I have a vivid recollection of a thrilling and anxious hour when, for the first time, I sailed a boat on the sea on my own.

While I love being on the water I hesitate to say that I always love the sea. I know from voyages under sail around the British Isles and across the North Atlantic how formidable it is. As well as exhilaration I have endured my share of seasickness and apprehension.

If the sea is not really lovable it nevertheless enthrals me for all sorts of reasons. It was where knowledge began. It is the heart of history, part of what we were and what we are.

The people of our islands have been, above all, seafarers, defined and inspired by the sea. It forms an unambiguous frontier. It has been our moat and also our magic carpet to the wider world. For four centuries it was our accomplice in empire. For many years we so commanded the seas through the Royal Navy and our huge merchant fleet that we allowed ourselves the conceit that we were virtual gods of the oceans. Our history, literature and language are soaked in salt water.

Wales has a wonderful and distinctive story as a maritime nation. Its face juts towards the Atlantic. The people living along its hundreds of miles of irregular and exposed coastline had perforce to engage with the sea. They lived by the dictates of the prevailing westerly winds and learned their business in the most difficult waters. It was a hard school from which they emerged as skilled sailors highly valued in a society whose fortune and livelihood depended on ships and seagoing professionals. They were, for example, much in demand in the great world port of Liverpool.

The graduates of this hard school included the remarkable tribe of Welsh sea captains who made the names of Jones, Roberts, Hughes, Llewellyn and Davies famous across the world. Welsh and Welsh accents were part of the clamour of teeming waterfronts in Sydney, Rio, Yokohama, Shanghai and countless other ports. Sailing into Valparaiso in Chile in 1906 the Welsh crew of the barque *Gwydyr Castle* found fifty ships in the harbour, twelve of them commanded by Welshmen and four of them, like the *Gwydyr Castle*'s captain, from the north Wales port of Nefyn. It was not an unusual event.

So the Roaring Forties seemed to blow along the quays of Wales. In towns up and down the coast thoughts turned frequently to the men at sea. Every day, wives and mothers anxiously scanned the shipping newspapers for information about the vessels on the other side of the world, ships manned by their husbands, fathers, brothers and sons. The significance of the sea is marked in churchyards all along the coast of Wales, on the numerous tombstones of respected captains, on the memorials to victims of shipwreck and on the cenotaph ledgers recording the lives of seamen who died far away.

Most crews included a boy or two. It made good sense. A seaman's skills necessarily had to be learnt from an early age, like a language. The only way to know the ropes was to grow up with ships and the sea; and thousands of Welsh lads did just that, thrilled to follow in grandfather's and father's footsteps – and aching to own a prized pair of German seaboots.

The sea was certainly an adventure, but we should beware of making too much of a poetic romance of it. In the sailing ship years especially, seamen endured lives that were often arduous and dangerous. We can imagine them, sardined in their cramped and wet quarters in the forecastle, grumbling about the stingy shipowners who carefully measured each penny spent, not least on food. Young Welshmen often went to sea because they saw little choice and hoped perhaps that seafaring would be better than the drudgery of life on a hill farm.

In the beginning was the ship; and the Welsh were skilled shipbuilders as well as sailors. Most of the vessels sailing from the small ports were locally built, financed with local money and manned by local men, carrying with them the hopes of their communities. Constructed on beaches without the aid of formal plans, fashioned by eye and the rule of thumb, they expressed the individuality of the modest men who made them.

At Aberaeron, in a harbour once filled with working sail, leisure craft await the tide

Before the mountains were penetrated by railways and roads – and there were few good roads to the sea until the early part of the twentieth century – ships were rugged seagoing trucks that sailed the coasts and delivered every imaginable commodity: food, timber, fertiliser, furniture and chapel organs.

Typically a hundred feet overall, the length of one and a half cricket pitches, the Welsh schooners of Victorian times were renowned for toughness. Look at the record of the Pwllheli-built *Theda*. In March 1888, commanded by Captain G.E. Dedwith, she sailed with a cargo of slates from Porthmadog to Hamburg. From there she went to Cadiz, what Porthmadog men called Cay-diz, filled her hold with salt and sailed across the Atlantic to Newfoundland. She went on to Labrador with general goods, loaded a new cargo of salted cod and headed back across the Atlantic. Favoured by strong winds, she reached Gibraltar in a record twelve days. She ran on to Patras in Greece to deliver her cod, a favourite food in many parts of the Mediterranean. From Greece she sailed to Casablanca, on the north African coast, to pick up a cargo of corn for South Shields in Northumberland. There she loaded coal for Waterford in Ireland and, after fourteen months at sea, her captain and six crew brought her home to Wales.

During the exploitation of the mineral wealth of Wales in the nineteenth century new harbours were built to ship out massive cargoes of coal and slate. The coal fed the hungry furnaces of steamships. Welsh steam coal was the Royal Navy's fuel of choice. Mountains of it were built up in ports and remote islands all over the world, strategic fuel stops for steamships; and much of it was delivered by sailing vessels. During the great Victorian transformation of Wales, the coal ports of Cardiff, Barry, Newport, Swansea and others, formed the energy centre of the world, their mining hinterland the generators of power and wealth. It must have seemed that the grimy workhorse ships would bustle in and out for ever. The north Wales quar-

Years of decline: Cardiff docks in the 1970s

ries dominated world slate production and roofed the rapidly-growing cities of Britain, Europe and elsewhere. The need to export slate created the ports and shipbuilding industries of Porthmadog and her sisters.

Sail and steam, merchant shipping, the ocean economy, the relentless struggle with the sea – these are the core of the story of seafaring Wales. But the drama has many other players. Inevitably, there are parasites, like the heartless wreckers who lured ships ashore and plundered them; and the pirates who were a constant menace and torment to sailors. A coast so pitted with remote coves was bound to be the haunt of smugglers, especially in years of swingeing and unpopular taxes; and there are plenty of stories of the brandy and tobacco runners who worked the night shift along the shores.

The sea ran through the lives of many other people, the shipbuilders, craftsmen, engineers, shipowners, emigration agents and the countless migrants who packed their hopes and scant possessions, said farewell to Wales, and faced the ordeal and lottery of the oceans to make new lives. Meanwhile, the lighthouse keepers maintained their vital warning lights in long vigils, and lifeboatmen buckled on their courage and headed into the storms. They all played their part in a tremendous and moving human story.

After many centuries the importance of the sea in our national life has diminished. In towns once devoted to ships, anchors are displayed on quayside plinths as keepsakes. Nevertheless, when we contemplate the sea we are drawn to our history and it remains an inspiration. It is there to dream on. And many thousands of us take to the sea, hoist the sails and seek adventure, challenge and, with any luck, fulfilment.

During the glorious summer days of filming *Fishlock's Sea Stories* for BBC Wales, we were fortunate to sail aboard the schooner *Kathleen and May*. She was built in Wales more than a century ago and endures as a living and lovely link to the epoch of working sail. She helped to connect us to the chronicles of a westward-facing people who voyaged to the planets of the distant oceans, built ships with an artist's eye, sailed them like heroes and left us a legacy of legends and, I would suggest, of self-respect ... our stimulating and dramatic tribal memories stowed in a sea chest.

Guiding light: the lighthouse at Nash Point, Glamorgan, stands 120 feet high and its beam can be seen more than 20 miles off

1. For Those in Peril

No wonder the wives of sailormen shivered when storms rattled their cottage windows on dark nights along the coast of Wales.

They had reason to fear the wind's howl and the sea's thunder. These are dangerous waters. A glance at a map shows that much of the coast is a lee shore to the prevailing winds blowing from the west and particularly the south-west. In other words, the gales drive vessels towards the land, especially hazardous in the age of sail when ships had no engines to help them work away from danger and lacked the accurate navigation instruments that modern seamen take for granted.

In 1807 it was shown that in St George's Channel, the stretch of sea between Wales and Ireland, for every ship wrecked on the Irish coast, ten were lost along the rocky shores of Wales.

This terrible trap for sailing ships was made more perilous by particularly fast-running tides, heavy swells and steep waves. From Llyn down to Pembrokeshire the coast offers few harbours of refuge in a westerly gale. Vicious reefs are littered with the bones of ships and sailormen.

Porth Neigwl earned its English name of Hell's Mouth for its notorious seas and numerous wrecks. The north coast is vulnerable in a north-westerly and the Skerries rocks, off Anglesey, form a fearsome trap. Few stretches of water in the world are as demanding of a seaman's abilities and knowledge as the Bristol Channel, the Severn Sea. The massive body of water moving from the Channel's wide mouth is squeezed into the narrows

Lee shore: the western bulwarks of Wales were particularly feared in the era of sail

and has nowhere to go but upwards. This extraordinary pressure produces the second-highest tidal range in the world, forty-five feet, with currents rushing at more than seven miles an hour. An outgoing tide setting against a south-westerly gale creates tumbling seas. As if that were not danger enough, sandbanks and shallow rock ledges seem like lurking crocodiles.

In October 1859 a violent storm hammered the coast of Wales, sank more than a hundred vessels and drowned hundreds of people. The steamship *Royal Charter* was driven ashore on Anglesey and 454 of her 495 passengers and crew were lost. Caught in the storm off Pembrokeshire, the captain of the Danish ship *Carolina* saw that his only chance was to run his ship into the narrow inlet of Porthgain. It took a cool nerve to steer through the boiling seas. The ship crashed into the jetty and the thirteen crew escaped by scrambling over the bowsprit. They were just in time. Within minutes their vessel was smashed to matchwood.

Tom Bennett, a local historian, told me the poignant story of the paddle steamer *Nimrod*, pounded to pieces at St David's Head four months later, with the loss of all forty-five on board. Tom showed me the piece of stern rail he recovered while diving on the wreck. 'Witnesses saw the distraught captain at the stern, holding this rail, the last person to touch it until I found it 140 years later.'

People who lived on the coast usually saw a shipwreck as a bounty and took what they could from the washed-up cargoes and timbers. Some of them tried to cause shipwrecks by lighting lamps to entice vessels onto the shore. To the perils of the sea, sailors had also to add the treachery of their fellow men, vultures in human form. 'There are stories of wreckers in Anglesey, Gower and Pembrokeshire,' Tom Bennett said. 'A light would be tied to an ox and moved slowly along the shore to persuade the crew of a ship at sea that they were seeing the light of a vessel in harbour and could safely come in. Then their ship would be wrecked. Everybody was at it, from the humble servants to the lords of the manor, fighting over the spoils.'

In contrast to the wreckers, lighthouses symbolised the ideal of protecting seafarers. Britain's dependence on sea trade demanded a defensive ring of coastal lights warning ships of rocks and shallows. Trinity House became the authority in charge of lighthouses, buoys and other navigation aids under an Act of Parliament in the reign of Queen Elizabeth I; but it is not well known that many early lighthouses were built privately to make big money from shipping fees. The most profitable private lighthouse in the world was the Smalls, twenty miles off the Pembrokeshire coast. Another big earner, charging ships a penny a ton, was the Skerries light, the vital guiding beacon for shipping in and out of Liverpool.

The owners of the Smalls and the Skerries fought hard to keep Trinity House from taking them over. One proprietor of the Smalls was a clergyman with a keen business mind. Trinity

House finally bought the lighthouse from him in 1836 for £170,000, a fortune; and secured the Skerries in 1841 for nearly £445,000, a huge sum and a monument to avarice.

A traditional story of the Smalls tells that when one of the two keepers died, his partner, afraid of being suspected of murder, decided to keep the body for autopsy. He put it in a simple coffin and hung it outside. But relief was a long time coming because of bad weather and the poor man, with only his dead friend for company, almost went mad. After this it was ruled that lighthouses should have three keepers.

Chris Williams once did a spell of duty on the Smalls. 'It really was small, too, with banana bunks curving around the walls, and if there were extra people on board, like an engineer, it could be cramped. But I loved the island lighthouses, like Flatholm, off Cardiff, and Lundy, off Devon. After all, one of the reasons I joined the service at eighteen was to work by the sea.'

British lighthouses are now automated and controlled from the Trinity House base in Harwich. Chris showed me around

Nash Point lighthouse, a guardian beacon in the dangerous Bristol Channel since the 1830s...

the Nash Point light on the Glamorgan coast where he used to be a keeper and where he now does routine servicing, changing the bulb, cleaning the glass, checking the batteries and standby generator. Built by Trinity House in 1832, after a ship was wrecked on the Nash Sands nearby, it was the last manned light in Wales and was automated in 1998.

Chris, evidently a congenial man, said: 'I loved the life. In general, keepers get on well. Very few arguments ever arose. On every station you always had a Bible and the *Guinness Book of Records* to settle any arguments. You lose your privacy but you are there of your own choosing, and if you don't like it you can leave.'

He took me up to the old light, a thick glass cylinder, large enough for both of us to stand in, essentially a huge magnifying glass or intensifier. The bulb was the size of a melon, 1,500 watts. The bulb in the modern automated system is the size of a car headlight bulb and only 150 watts, but its range of more than twenty miles is almost as great as the old light.

... it also has a big voice – the huge, earth-trembling foghorns can be heard for twenty miles

When the visibility is bad the lighthouse has the back-up of a fog signal, the great trombone of south Wales. Chris showed me the foghorn house with its two mighty horns on the roof. 'You start a diesel engine that drives a compressor that forces air into a tank that blows through a reed and makes the deep resonating sound that can be heard for twenty miles. You feel the building tremble, the vibration coming through your feet.'

Many lighthouses, especially those on exposed rocks out at sea, represent amazing feats of engineering and construction. Standing guard over the most dangerous traps, they certainly made the sailor's life safer. But as shipping increased shipwrecks were unfortunately a commonplace. Until the 1820s, little was done to save the passengers and crews of ships driven ashore. Crowds watched in helpless horror as ships were smashed on the rocks, often tantalisingly close to the land.

The Royal National Lifeboat Institution, the world's first sea rescue service, was founded in 1824. Around that time, too,

To the rescue: the Moelfre lifeboat *Robert and Violet* off the coast of Anglesey

lifeboats were organized informally by coastal communities in Wales. A lifeboat association was started in Anglesey by the Reverend James Williams, rector of Llanfairynghornwy, after he witnessed a shipwreck on the island coast. Such harrowing events often led local people to vow that 'something must be done.' The Anglesey association opened a station in the village of Moelfre in the 1840s with a boat propelled by six oars. Since then Moelfre men have saved more than 700 lives.

Moelfre, I think, is typical of lifeboat communities. The lifeboat is the heart of the village and the focus of intense local pride. You only have to visit a local pub and look at all the photographs of lifeboats and their crews to see how important it is.

I went out for a few hours in Moelfre's Tyne-class boat *Robert and Violet*, one of the world's most advanced rescue craft, forty-seven feet and made of steel, her twin diesels giving seventeen knots, twice the speed of earlier designs. Today she would cost a million pounds. A lifeboat launch is always thrilling. We rumbled down the slipway and splashed into the sea, a far cry from the days when many lifeboats in Wales were launched into the surf from carriages hauled by men or horses.

The station has two full-time employees, the coxswain and the mechanic. As we headed out to sea, Anthony Barclay, coxswain for five years, told me that every lifeboatman feels he has a tradition to live up to. 'When I was growing up in Moelfre joining the lifeboat was every lad's ambition. When the maroons went off we used to run down to watch the lifeboat going out, especially on a rough day. We just wanted to be part of it. Someone asked my mother if I would like to join, when I was about seventeen, and that was it.

'The boat needs a crew of six and we have around twenty-six people to call on. There's no shortage of volunteers. We do very well for a small village. We're a family and everyone sticks together. We still use the maroons to call people out but we rely mainly on our pagers. Every time the pager goes off or the

Proud to be part of a long tradition, Anthony Barclay is coxswain of the Moelfre lifeboat

maroons go up you still get that buzz. We're usually in the water in less than ten minutes.

'Training is intensive. Electronics are great but don't always mix with sea water, so the first thing we teach the crew is basic navigation on a paper chart. When I joined, most of the crew were seamen, in the Merchant Navy or working on fishing boats. But today fewer people go to sea for a living. They have no seafaring background so we teach them from scratch. What makes a good lifeboatman is dedication, being prepared to drop everything when your pager goes off. Yes, your life may be on the line, but you never really think about it.'

Moelfre's lifeboat secretary, Ifan Jones, told me of the hurricane of 1959 and an epic of the Moelfre lifeboat. She was launched to save the crew of the Cardiff freighter *Hindlea* which was being driven towards the Anglesey rocks and

Local hero: Dick Evans was one of the great lifeboatmen. As coxswain of the Moelfre lifeboat he won RNLI Gold Medals for daring rescues in 1959 and 1967

pounded by waves twenty-five feet high. There was not a minute to spare. Coxswain Dick Evans steered around the stern of the ship which was pitching so wildly that her propeller was sometimes out of the water and rotating above the lifeboat crew's heads. A huge wave rolled the lifeboat onto her side, and another hurled her into the *Hindlea*'s hull. One of the ship's crew leapt to the lifeboat. Time and again the battered lifeboat closed with the ship to rescue the crew of eight one by one, the last man grabbed just before the ship was driven ashore and wrecked. Dick Evans won a gold medal for seamanship and courage that day and his crew were also decorated. Seven years later, in another hurricane-force storm, Dick Evans and the acting coxswain of the Holyhead lifeboat won gold medals for a joint rescue of the crew of a Greek steamer. Dick Evans served with the Moelfre boat for forty-nine years.

Lifeboatmen possess local knowledge that can mean the difference between life and death. So, too, do the pilots. At the end

Bristol Channel pilot cutters were among the fastest and toughest sailing vessels. The mainsail insignia identifies a Barry pilot

of a long voyage a ship's crew was comforted by the sight of a familiar headland or lighthouse. They were almost home but not quite. The last stage of a voyage is usually the most dangerous. So the captain engaged the services of a pilot to guide him into port. In the days of sail pilots went out to meet incoming ships in their fast and robust cutters, vessels specially designed for such work.

Tom Cunliffe, an author and seaman, long ago fell in love with, and owned, a Bristol Channel pilot cutter built for a Barry pilot in 1911; and when the time came to replace her he had a replica built. As I discovered, she is beautiful and a joy to handle.

'Between the Bristol Channel pilots there was cut-throat competition,' Tom said. 'There was big money at stake. They worked as individuals, racing out to westward to meet ships.

Race for glory: a Cardiff pilot cutter, right, hard on the heels of a rival from Barry

Sometimes it was neck and neck. The first pilot to get to a ship hove-to and asked the captain what port he was bound for. "Barry," he might say. An apprentice rowed the pilot to the ship and the pilot was welcomed aboard. The crack pilots made a lot of money. Lewis Alexander of Barry could make £1,000 a year and that went a long way in 1911. You could get a smart house for £200 and a new pilot cutter for £400. The pilots were well worth their fees. Given the nature of the Bristol Channel they had to be the best. They had huge responsibilities, were out in all weathers, and ships' cargoes were very valuable.'

Well into the twentieth century, when most ships were driven by engines, the Bristol Channel pilots remained loyal to their sailing cutters and worked as individuals, every man for himself. It was partly a matter of independence. They knew their cutters: they were more comfortable, faster and reliable than boats with steam engines. Some of the modern-minded pilots who went over to steam were infuriated to find themselves outstripped by the sailing cutters in the race to the west.

But everything changed around the time of the First World War. The pilots were made to work together and to give up sail. With the advent of radio, ships could book a pilot in advance. The wonderful age of the swashbuckling racing pilots was over.

Pilots, of course, guide ships out of ports as well as in, setting them on their way before wishing the captain bon voyage and transferring to their pilot launch to return to base. As a rule the Liverpool pilots leave their ships off the coast of Anglesey. Sometimes, however, bad weather has made it impossible for a pilot to transfer to his boat and he has taken an involuntary voyage across the Atlantic, next stop New York.

The sea always has the last word. For many years the struggle was to make seafaring safer with better navigation, better equipment, better ships. But every seafarer knows that the sea never changes and always finds the gaps in our defences.

The iniquitous slave trade and the West Indies sugar plantations made fortunes for many British merchants. Liverpool was a major beneficiary of the business.

2. The Welsh Navy

From the eighteenth century into the twentieth the great ocean city of Liverpool so hummed with Welsh voices that Welsh people imagined it a capital of Wales.

Only twenty miles from the northern border of Wales it was a natural magnet for labour, talent and goods and a particular attraction for seafaring men. In a relationship of mutual benefit Wales became part of the story of Liverpool; and Liverpool a chapter in the story of Wales.

Welsh fisheries, farms and quarries shipped cargoes of salted herrings, butter, corn, cattle, stone and slate to Liverpool. Craftsmen went to build the fabric of the fast-growing city. Businessmen settled and set up shops, shipping lines and publishing houses. A distinctive Liverpool Welsh community, Welsh-speaking and amply garrisoned by chapels, emerged as a bourgeoisie with considerable influence in the cultural and political affairs of Victorian and Edwardian Wales.

The core of the matter was always the sea.

The former fishing village of Liverpool began to grow into a substantial port early in the eighteenth century. From the 1760s it flourished on the profits of the African slave business and, as a slave trade port, outstripped London and Bristol. In the triangular trade, ships sailed from the Mersey to West Africa with copper, iron, woollens and guns, carried slaves across the Atlantic to the West Indies and America, and returned to Britain with sugar, tobacco and rum.

Maritime might: Welsh seafarers flocked to Liverpool and helped to make it a great port

The British craving for sugar was insatiable. Hundreds of sugarcane-crushing windmills dotted the Barbados landscape. Today only one survives, the Morgan Lewis mill built by a Welsh planter. Britain, France, Spain, the Netherlands and the United States were major slave traders and over the centuries carried around eleven million Africans, rounded up and sold by African kings and merchants, across the Atlantic. In the 1790s British ships were running fifty thousand slaves a year to the plantations which generated four-fifths of Britain's overseas income.

Profits were not confined to a few tycoons. Many modest businessmen, tailors, grocers and barbers, invested in slave voyages. Earnings financed shipbuilding, sail and rope making and much else. The Liverpool merchant, Richard Pennant, later Lord Penrhyn, ploughed his Jamaican sugar profits into vast estates in North Wales and built a slate quarrying empire that doubled his fortune. Penrhyn Castle, built in the 1820s, stands as a monument to the economic power generated by sugar and the sweat of slaves. William Gladstone of Hawarden, four times Prime Minister, never forgot that his family's fortunes came from the iniquitous trade.

By the time Britain outlawed the slave trade in 1807 Liverpool was an Atlantic gateway, the chief port for American cotton imports, reaping the benefit of its investment in docks. The defeat of Napoleonic France in 1815 ended more than twenty gruelling years of war, made Britain supreme at sea and ushered in a new prosperity based on the Atlantic trade. Britain commanded the lion's share of world shipping throughout the century. Liverpool's coterie of shrewd shipowners made their city the bustling and broad-shouldered counterpart of New York. They also made their London cousins look soft.

It was Liverpool merchants who, in the 1820s, built Britain's first commercial telegraph, ten semaphore stations along the North Wales coast which relayed messages from Holyhead to

Point Lynas on the north coast of Anglesey: once part of Liverpool's sema-phore early warning system

Liverpool in five minutes. When ships were sighted their names were flashed along to Liverpool and the owners knew that their rich cargoes were safe and they could begin to count the profits.

These owners depended, of course, on the skill and experience of the men who manned their ships. Seasoned Welsh seamen who had learnt their ship-handling in the currents and storms along the coast of Wales were highly-regarded and much sought-after. 'They were prized for their knowledge and ability,' said Captain Gwyn Pari Huws, a master mariner and for many years the marine superintendent at Liverpool. 'They quickly graduated to be masters of large sailing ships on the deep-sea routes. They also became shipping company managers and owners.'

As we watched sailing vessels using their engines to manoeuvre into Liverpool's Canning Dock, Gwyn reminded me that sailing ship men would work the winds and tides, perhaps at night, with no power except their sails.

'How they managed in bad weather, I don't know. But it's probably fair to say that they didn't know it was difficult. They had been brought up with it, of course. A schooner would bring slate from north Wales, for example, without instruments, power or a pilot, just two men and a boy. They really were a remarkable breed. Their sea clothes were much the same as those they wore ashore. And the victualling was primitive – it was a treat if the skipper added a pig's head to the menu.'

More than one shipping company hired so many men from Wales that it was known as the Welsh Navy.

One of these was the Ocean Steamship Company, known as the Blue Funnel Line, founded in 1865 by the shipping tycoon Alfred Holt. As an engineer he developed more efficient engines and propellers, making ships more profitable as well as safer. And he pioneered the long-distance steamer. His son Lawrence created better facilities for seamen, including an education and library service for merchant sailors. Parents took their sons to see him at his holiday home in Llyn and he gave

Entering a dock in Liverpool, the skipper has the blessing of his reliable engine. Old timers had to rely on their sailing skills

the boys a chit to take to Birkenhead where they could start as apprentices or deck boys.

Shipowners and merchants from Wales fitted in well with the business climate in Liverpool because they were Nonconformist, said Dr Alan Scarth of the Liverpool Maritime Museum. 'The spirit of the times in the nineteenth century was to marry honesty with business. Chapels formed a network. Going to church was not only a religious experience.'

Many Welsh shipowners sprang from families known for religious and business zeal. The marine historian Aled Eames went so far as to write that such men were often associated with incredible meanness, that they sat 'piously in their chapels and shook their heads when they heard the complaints and tragedies relating to their ships and the men whose toil brought them the profits which enabled them to build their fine houses and many chapels.'

One of the great human dynamics of the Victorian age was migration, the surge of millions of hopeful people out of Europe, squeezing into ships, their minds full of fear and dreams.

Until the middle of the nineteenth century most Welsh migrants were from the countryside, said Dr Bill Jones, of Cardiff University. They were acutely aware of the shortage of land and high rents at home and attracted by the promise of free land in America.

'After that, most migrants were industrial workers with the skills that America wanted. Society in late nineteenth-century Wales was mobile, not static, and migration was a factor for many people. Most went in the hope that they would have better lives. Emigration was a very carefully planned move for the majority in which they weighed the options of staying or going.'

People sailed from all the little ports of Wales. In Caernarfon, for example, ships loaded slate, filled the space between the cargo and the deck with migrants, and sailed off to Boston, Quebec and New York.

'But as the emigration business grew,' said Bill Jones, 'it became centred on Liverpool, particularly with the change from sail to steam. Rail links helped, too, with emigrant trains leaving south Wales for Liverpool every Monday. Newspapers wrote of emigration fever. Many migrants used emigration agents, who themselves had representatives in Welsh towns, a newspaper proprietor or grocer, and arranged tickets and travel. Some agents were reputed to be unreliable or tricksters, so much so that in the 1870s the emigration agent Gomer Roberts promised in his newspaper advertisement to meet his customers sober and to put them on the right ship.'

Many ships carried eight hundred or so passengers, the equivalent of two modern jumbo jets. 'They met new people, cultures and lifestyles, all the variety of America, as soon as they boarded.'

For most migrants, the cheap-ticket passengers in the steerage, the Atlantic was a fearful ordeal. Shipowners crammed

Sick, wet, packed thigh-by-thigh with their neighbours, emigrants often endured a rough Atlantic crossing to reach the promised land

them aboard like herrings in a barrel and they lived in cramped, ratty and stinking squalor, 'conditions worse than the dark ages,' said one captain. For many years they had to provide their own food and never knew how long they would be at sea. One company told its passengers to bring straw bedding, two hams, potatoes, flour, tea and sugar, as well as pots and pans. Conditions were so bad that Parliament passed a law forcing owners to provide a food ration, a modicum of humanity in a decidedly unsentimental business.

To the fury of the ocean was added the horror of typhus, dysentery and cholera which killed passengers by the dozen. No year was worse than 1847. One twelfth of the 105,000 people who sailed for Quebec from Liverpool and Cork died at sea or in quarantine within sight of Quebec. Of 476 passengers who sailed from Liverpool in the *Virginius* in May 268 perished.

In 1866 Jonathan Edwards wrote to his brother in Rhymney describing a terrible Atlantic voyage from Liverpool aboard a steamship carrying hundreds of passengers. He wrote of storms, hunger and cholera. The tone was set by the first meal on board - 'You at home often give better food to the pigs.'

As cholera began to strike, he wrote in his diary: 'Death is using his sword very easily now and a more frightening storm than any we have seen has sprung up. Two died last night and six today.' In the following days he recorded: 'Six died last night ... Five died last night and two at midday. It is extremely heart-breaking with our fellow emigrants groaning so with cramp and dying so suddenly ... Seven died today but we are not sure whether they are all dead or not, but we are sure they are thrown overboard without ceremony ... Our hearts bled to see our friends dying. There was a woman crying bitterly having seen her baby thrown into the sea.'

He graphically described the violence among the frightened and desperate passengers. 'The Germans and the Irish have been drawing their knives on each other. The two sides were like dogs.'

Cholera killed fifty of the passengers in a week and fifty sick were taken off at New York. Food was delivered on board and 'the men were like hungry lions leaping over each other and snarling. Many were nearly crushed to death; others were cursing and hitting each other.'

William Evans sailed from Liverpool in 1853 in a ship that took seven weeks to cross the Atlantic. He wrote that terrified passengers pleaded with the captain to turn back; but he sailed on.

Robert Williams, who left from Liverpool in 1844, wrote of storms, sickness, men brawling and slums below decks. 'It is almost impossible to imagine the appearance of the people aboard, their clothes in rags and their caps as if they had been a living room for bugs and fleas.'

But it was worth all the suffering to reach New York. 'I never saw such a wonderful place. Independence is seen on every face, not scared and frightened of bishop or priest. Surprisingly, few children are seen in the streets as they are in Wales. They are sent to school and all of them are free ... and they give their opinions with boldness of grown men. Although they are young they are listened to earnestly. The farmers of Wales would be amazed to see the tables of the poor spread with five to ten courses every meal.'

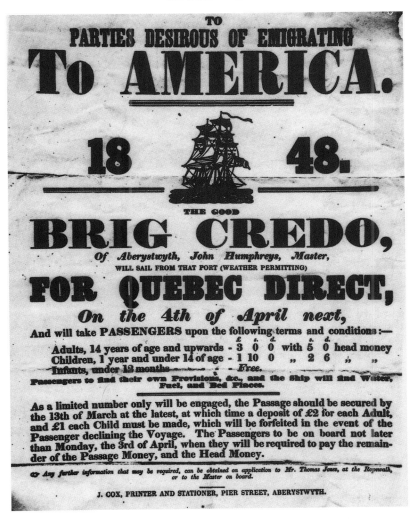

TO PARTIES DESIROUS OF EMIGRATING

TO AMERICA.

18 **48.**

THE GOOD

BRIG CREDO,

Of Aberystwyth, John Humphreys, Master,

WILL SAIL FROM THAT PORT (WEATHER PERMITTING)

FOR QUEBEC DIRECT,

On the 4th of April next,

And will take PASSENGERS upon the following terms and conditions :—

Adults, 14 years of age and upwards - 3 0 0 with 5 0 head money
Children, 1 year and under 14 of age - 1 10 0   „   2 6   „   „
Infants, under 12 months —— . - Free.

Passengers to find their own Provisions, &c., and the Ship will find Water, Fuel, and Bed Places.

As a limited number only will be engaged, the Passage should be secured by the 13th of March at the latest, at which time a deposit of £2 for each Adult, and £1 each Child must be made, which will be forfeited in the event of the Passenger declining the Voyage. The Passengers to be on board not later than Monday, the 3rd of April, when they will be required to pay the remainder of the Passage Money, and the Head Money.

☞ *Any further information that may be required, can be obtained on application to Mr. Thomas Jones, at the Ropewalk, or to the Master on board.*

J. COX, PRINTER AND STATIONER, PIER STREET, ABERYSTWYTH.

In 1840 the Nova Scotian merchant Samuel Cunard founded his Atlantic steamship line with a service between Liverpool and Boston. As Liverpool grew in importance Cunard ran the leading transatlantic passenger service.

In the 1850s men discovered gold in Australia and tens of thousands clamoured to get there, many of them from Wales.

Gateway to the world: Liverpool grew as the counterpart to New York

Some smart shipowners in Liverpool introduced a new class of fast ship and made Liverpool the chief European port for Australia. Their ships cut the voyage to three and a half months and one skipper raced to Melbourne in seventy-four days. The authorities would not believe it until he produced a newspaper he had bought in Liverpool on the day he sailed.

'An Atlantic crossing might take six weeks, but the passage to Australia up to five months,' said Bill Jones, 'but the conditions on the Australia run were better because migrants were on assisted passages, their fares paid for by the government or charitable bodies, and there was an interest in delivering them in good condition.'

Liverpool was a city of farewells, none more poignant than that of the party that assembled on the dockside in May 1865. More than one hundred and sixty men, women and children boarded the sailing ship *Mimosa* to voyage to the earth's ends

Off to Patagonia in the morning: the *Mimosa* etched its name in Welsh history

to found a Welsh colony in Patagonia. Chief among those seeing them off was Michael D. Jones, the Bala preacher and patriarchal figure in Welsh nationalism, who organized and partly financed the expedition. Patagonia was his dream, a new Wales beyond the seas, whose culture and language would be protected by distance and isolation.

The *Mimosa*'s striking female figurehead was apparently too female for some of the organizers (there was a sailorly tradition that a bare-breasted figure calmed the seas) and it was replaced by a simple scroll.

The pioneers were mostly from the south Wales coalfield, fifty-six married people in their thirties, sixty-one children, thirty or so bachelors and a dozen single women in their twenties. They sang a patriotic song and sailed away. It was as if they were going to another planet. We can imagine their emotions, most of them knowing they would never see their friends and families again. It took two months to reach their destination. During the voyage a widow and widower married each other, four children died and two were born.

The migrants thought they were off to a garden of Eden, but

Familiar to countless Welsh sailors, the River Mersey

their expedition was so poorly thought-out that they struggled through years of hardship. Lewis Jones, who had been out to scout the territory, had returned to Wales with a misleadingly optimistic picture of a fertile promised land. An advance party of two men had gone out to prepare the way but there was little they could do in what looked like a wilderness. Only two of the pioneers had any idea of farming. The migrants were saved by the native people, who showed them how to hunt and survive, and by the Argentine government which sent food. In the end, though, they prospered modestly; and Welsh is still spoken in Patagonia. The last large group of Welsh migrants to the colony, more than a hundred, sailed from Liverpool in 1911.

Meanwhile, with the building of more docks and the huge Cammell Laird shipbuilding yards across the Mersey in Birkenhead, Liverpool became one of the largest seaports of the world, vigorous and confident, filled with freighters and lofty glamorous liners. As sailors and shipowners, builders and merchants, Welsh people contributed their unique flavour to an adventurous cosmopolitan society. Although a transplanted community, they were self-consciously proud of their origins and culture. They wrestled with the problems of subsuming their identity in the great Atlantic city. But they were there because they had much to offer. They also had much to gain.

Centenarian: the Welsh schooner *Kathleen and May*

3. The Forests of Ships

The coast of Wales was a hazy blue smudge on the horizon when I took the wheel of the schooner *Kathleen and May*. She was very good-tempered about it, almost a living creature, full of grace.

She was built in Wales more than a century ago and I wondered how many men over the years had stood on this deck, holding the wheel spokes, looking up at the tan sails and watching the bowsprit dipping gently.

Her seakindly lines and the way she moved through the water showed that she was a thoroughbred, still a dancer in the breeze, a survivor of the long age of the workaday sailing ships.

Kathleen and May is certainly a tribute to her builders. Just under a hundred feet long and a hundred tons, she was launched at Ferguson and Baird's yard in Connah's Quay in Flintshire in April 1900, and cost £2,700. Like all such vessels she was strongly made for a life of hard work. Her heavy oak frames were planked with three-inch thick pine. Bunks for four hands were fitted in the forecastle and small cabins aft for the captain and the mate. The hold had space for almost two hundred and thirty tons of cargo; and for sixty years the ship carried loads of bricks, cement, coal and pitch between Wales, Scotland, Ireland, the west of England and the Channel Islands.

Once there were hundreds of schooners like her, built on beaches and riverbanks at Mostyn, Conwy, Beaumaris, Amlwch, Holyhead, Bangor, Caernarfon, Nefyn, Pwllheli,

Porthmadog, Barmouth, Aberdyfi, Aberystwyth, Aberaeron, New Quay, Cardigan, Milford Haven, Tenby, Llanelli, Porthcawl, Newport and Chepstow.

The timber from which they were built was often cut in nearby forests. Long before iron and steel, shipbuilders walked in their local woodlands to find their timber, the beams and ribs, seeing the shapely curves of their ships in the living oaks.

Twm Elias showed me the woodland at Borth y Gest, near Porthmadog, full of oaks planted more than a century ago to build schooners. It was never harvested because wooden ship-building came to an end. 'Look closely,' said Twm, 'and you can see the trees growing in the shape of the timbers the ship-wrights and carpenters were looking for. Timber with a natural shape was much stronger than pieces bolted or glued together. They didn't have superglue in those days. They were looking

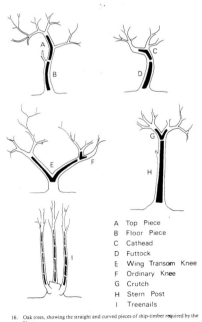

A Top Piece
B Floor Piece
C Cathead
D Futtock
E Wing Transom Knee
F Ordinary Knee
G Crutch
H Stern Post
I Treenails

16. Oak trees, showing the straight and curved pieces of ship-timber required by the Navy.

All in the eye of the shipwright: the ribs and frames of ships grew in the woods

Centuries of experience: the ship takes shape on the shore

for the curve of a rib, a wing or a knee. And in the woods they also found the material for the wooden pegs used for fastening the timbers, immensely strong.'

Using tools hardly changed in centuries, the shipwrights chipped and chiselled the frames, the ship's curved bones growing from the keel.

The Welsh schooners were perhaps the finest small merchant sailing ships ever built. Those constructed along the coast between Bangor, Caernarfon and Porthmadog in the nineteenth century were the response to the problem of exporting slate. Porthmadog, which flourished from 1825 until the First World War, was created by slate. The narrow-gauge railway brought huge quantities down from Blaenau Ffestiniog to the waiting ships. The slate industry's rapid expansion, said Owain T. P. Roberts, a marine archaeologist, created a demand for fast and rugged ships that could carry around three hundred tons of slates and sail their way off treacherous lee shores. The fore-and-aft schooner rig on two or three masts was ideal, enabling a vessel to sail closer to the wind and claw her way to the open sea against the prevailing wind. There were no engines, of course, and a ship had to be completely independent.

The wonder of such schooners is that they evolved, not from a drawing board and scientific calculations, but from the crafts-man's eye and judgment. 'It is not a myth that the schooners were built by eye,' said Owain Roberts. 'The traditional way was for the shipbuilder to make a model of half a hull and he and the owner agreed on the shape.'

In Caernarfon, Captain Gwyn Pari Huws showed me one of the few surviving ship half-models. It was used to build the *Pride of Wales*. It looked beautiful, more than four feet long and curved like a cello, made of vertical wooden slices so that the whole hull model was like a sliced loaf. Gwyn pulled out a segment and demonstrated how the shipwrights, working on the floor of a loft, scaled up the pieces to build the full-scale timbers of a ship. 'From 1820 to 1913 more than two hundred Porthmadog ships were built from half-models like this,' he said, 'and such models are rare today because once a vessel was built the model was thrown away.'

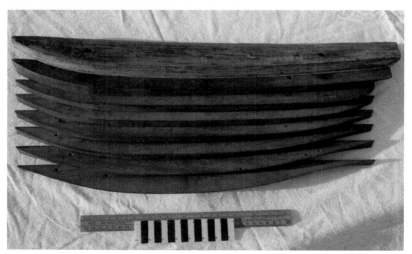

Using sections of the hull model as their pattern, shipbuilders constructed beautiful vessels

Owain Roberts once examined a half-model from the 1880s and ran its lines through his calculator.

'She was perfect and could not be improved on. Yet the builder had no drawing board and probably did not know how to calculate displacement. It was absolutely remarkable, done totally by experience and eye. He built a ship he knew would float and this knowledge came from ships he had built earlier. Before that, he had learnt his craft as an apprentice to a shipbuilder, drawing on another man's experience, on generations of knowledge. Their traditions gave shipbuilders a good sense of what made a ship work. And since they built ships of around a hundred feet they did not confront the problems of stress and strain that come with ships of greater size.'

He pointed out that while many ships were excellent performers we do not know how many were indifferent. 'But you could tweak a sailing ship a bit, play around with extra ballast, extra weight. The tweaking process could take a long time, perhaps months, and that could be an expensive business.

'The schooners were strong and solidly built, as they had to be to carry a dead weight of slate and stand up to the stresses of the sea. And they were manned by experienced men. If you started at thirteen you eventually got to know every trick. In the big ocean-going ships there was a preference for young men who had served in Welsh schooners. Their abilities were highly valued.'

When *Kathleen and May* was built in 1900 sailing ships were still good business propositions. There was what we would call today a thriving niche market. For all the advantages of vessels driven by steam engines, sailing ships remained economical and useful well into the twentieth century. They were reliable and there was no fuel bill; and since they were manned by a handful of men the wages were low. A photograph of 1901 shows thirty-nine schooners drying their sails in the sheltered harbour at Holyhead.

Victorian New Quay had three shipbuilding beaches, Cei Bach, Traeth Gwyn and New Quay itself, separately listed in Lloyd's register of shipping

'The railways sounded the knell for the coastal schooners,' said Owain Roberts, 'but it's probably true that the First World War put an end to them. They were sitting ducks for German submarines. They could not escape and were sunk by gunfire. Had there been no war the sailing vessels might have gone on for another twenty years.'

Shipbuilding was often financed by local communities. The cost was divided into sixty-four shares and these were often sub-divided so that a vessel might be owned by hundreds of local investors. The builder, the owner and the master had shares and others were bought by farmers and shopkeepers.

'Some Methodist ministers invested quite heavily in ships and one or two became famous for their ship-owning rather than their preaching,' said the historian Dr Geraint Jenkins. 'The whole community was involved. The ships locally built, locally manned, brought in all the necessities of life, lime to fertilize the land, drainage tiles, the chapel organ. It's not easy for

Along the coast of Wales the names of pubs speak of seafaring history. The *Cadwgan* sailed out of Aberaeron for many years

us today to appreciate just how remote the Ceredigion coast was for many years. Along here ships were the lifeline. The roads were poor and the mountains difficult so that it was far easier to bring goods by sea.'

In many coastal towns and villages the seafaring past is commemorated in the names of streets and houses. Retired captains built houses and named them after a favourite ship. In Aberaeron the Cadwgan hotel is named after a famous vessel. New Quay has many such fine houses, in keeping with its maritime history. 'It was an important shipbuilding town,' Geraint Jenkins said. 'They built around three hundred ships here and many sailed all over the world. And then there were the supporting industries, the blacksmiths, foundries, riggers, block makers, rope makers, sailmakers – so many sailmakers that they had their own brass band. It's not easy to work out who did what because so many of them were Davieses.'

Geraint Jenkins is a native of Llangrannog where about twenty-four ships were built on the beach. Generations of seafarers sail through his ancestry. His great-grandfather was

Like many Welsh villages Llangrannog bred ocean-going men

known for his obstinacy as Joseph yr Asyn, Joseph the Donkey – 'a pillar of Bancyfelin chapel and of the Pentre Arms, a vast drinker of beer who lived to ninety-three, owned three ships and lost them in a gale. His four sons were sailors who all lost their lives at sea, off Java, Rio, the Scillies and Ireland. My great-uncle Elias sailed from here at the age of nine, as deck boy and trainee cook, first stop East Africa.

'Ports like this were outward looking. They were also female communities because men were at sea. The women congregated at the shipping office in Llangrannog every day to read Lloyd's List and they would see that their husbands' ships were in Fremantle or Yokohama or other places.'

Traditional methods of on-the-beach shipbuilding persisted in other parts of the world long after they were discontinued in Wales. Thirty years ago the Pembrokeshire yachtsman Val Howells skippered a schooner in the West Indies and studied shipbuilding there. It was a little like Victorian Porthmadog, but with coconuts and calypso. 'They were building on the fore-shore just as we used to, vessels built to earn someone a living, with beautiful lines and made like a church out of high quality timber. When you create a boat and do the design yourself there aren't any straight lines.'

He smiled. 'If you have a good curve on your thumb you get a nicely curved boat.'

Val Howells went to sea as a teenager in the Merchant Service and was in one of the supporting ships at the invasion of Normandy in 1944: after a few days it hit a mine and was towed home for repair. He brought his years of seafaring experience to the problems of building boats for single-handed voyaging. He competed in the first solo transatlantic race in 1960, in a twenty-five foot wooden Folkboat. The race was won by Francis Chichester. Val Howells competed again in 1964. He built his own glass fibre yacht for the 1976 race but broke his leg while constructing her. He had not fully recovered when he started the race and had to give up off the Irish coast. Eventually his health failed. But he still had sea fever and

A former midshipman in the 'Welsh navy', Val Howells is a consummate seaman, ocean sailor and raconteur

Aboard *Kathleen and May*: such a ship could be sailed by a handful of men and a boy

achieved his dream of sailing around the world alone, a three-year voyage.

He was a figure in a simpler, more modest, and perhaps more romantic, age of single-handed voyaging. 'The first solo Atlantic was a shoestring event, frowned on by the yachting establishment because it was feared it might bring yachting into disrepute. By 1976 it was becoming a professional game, with sponsorship and big money involved, outside the spirit of the first races which celebrated the amateur ideal.'

Certainly construction has come a long way since Val Howells and his fellow Corinthians dared the Atlantic in their small wooden boats forty or so years ago. Aboard the *Kathleen and May*, I reflected that in many ways he was much closer to those doughty Welsh shipbuilders who felled their trees, cleared a space on the beach, ensured that their thumbs had a nice curve and built as their grandfathers had taught them.

Modern yachts are made of materials those old boys could not dream of – titanium, carbon fibre, stainless steel, glass fibre – electronic spaceship stuff, precisely engineered, computer-drawn. Advanced instruments and satellites handle much of the navigation. Those Porthmadog and New Quay men who sailed the oceans in, more or less, the clothes they wore on the quay-side, would be astonished by the advanced warm and weatherproof gear worn by today's seafarers. But some things cannot change. Timber or steel, a ship is still a ship and the sea is still the implacable sea.

4. From Wales to the World

First they had to dig the coal, then they had to get it to the world. Much of the history of Wales is founded on the great mineral wealth lying under the surface of its mountains and valleys. The sea story is a crucial part of it.

During the nineteenth century businessmen constructed grand new harbours to ship out massive cargoes of coal and slate. Cardiff, Barry, Swansea, Newport and others were gateways to the oceans and key players in Britain's industrial transformation.

A sail on the Cleddau. For hundreds of years small vessels carried cargoes to and from small ports along the river

Working sail: *Kathleen and May* loading coal at Pembroke in the early twentieth century

These Victorian titans were in striking contrast to the local ports which had grown up from medieval times as part of the coastal transport network. Some of them had a modest industrial history. The Cleddau river in Pembrokeshire, for example, was for centuries a trading route plied by small sailing vessels working the tides, delivering corn, oysters, timber, stone and fuel.

'Pembrokeshire was the earliest coalfield worked in Wales,' Robert Scourfield told me. 'Anthracite was mined in small pits and shipped out from Creswell Quay from the thirteenth century. As places like London grew, the value of coal increased

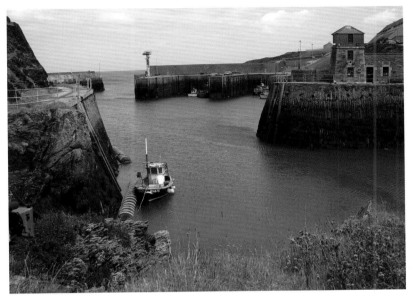

Amlwch, leaning on its long history

and local landowners dug more coal and shipped it out. Limestone was also exported, and so was culm, the precursor of smokeless fuel, which was coal dust mixed with estuary mud or clay and compressed into bricks. It made a wonderful cooking fire.'

The pocket-sized harbour of Amlwch in Anglesey made its mark in industrial history and grew rich on the copper hacked from Parys Mountain, two miles away. In 1768 prospectors investigating the old Roman workings discovered a mass of copper, the largest reserve then known in the world.

Thomas Williams, a shrewd local lawyer, became mine manager and, in time, the boss of the entire British copper industry. He was one of the outstanding British businessmen of the eighteenth century. He developed his sea and canal transport to move the copper and built a giant smelting works at Holywell in Flintshire. He ran the trade at a time of huge demand from shipowners and the Royal Navy for their ships to be copper-bottomed, the hulls covered with thin sheets of copper. This served two vital purposes: it protected ships from the dangerous tropical teredo worm that burrowed into ships' timbers and destroyed them; and it inhibited the growth of barnacles and weed that created drag and made ships slow. Coppered ships were faster, safer, steered better and saved big dockyard repair bills. Anglesey copper helped to ensure that the British navy ruled the seas.

For Thomas Williams, Parys Mountain was better than a gold mine. Not for nothing was he known as the Copper King. His rivals saw him as the most ruthless of businessmen and called him a despot. His workers knew him as a decent boss and awarded him the affectionate nickname of Twm Chwarae Teg, Tom Fair Play.

As for Amlwch, it was a hardship post for preachers, a wild and seething boom town with sixty pubs and mobs of miners brawling beneath the stinking yellow cloud emitted by the thirty-one smelters. When the great copper seam was at last exhausted in the nineteenth century, as pitted with tunnels and holes as a rabbit warren, Amlwch turned to shipbuilding and launched some famous schooners.

Cardiff, too, had modest beginnings. It grew in the industrial revolution and soared to success in the iron age of the nineteenth century as the outlet for the rails manufactured in Merthyr Tydfil and elsewhere. The rails were shipped to the fast-expanding railways of the world, in Russia, the United States and the British empire.

In 1839 the second Marquess of Bute built the dock that established Cardiff as a major port. Twelve years later, the Admiralty decreed that coal from south Wales, renowned for producing great heat, was perfect for the steam-driven warships then being developed. The Royal Navy's endorsement opened a huge world market for this wonder fuel and Cardiff became emphatically a capital of coal and shipowning.

Cardiff in the 1970s: waiting for the tide to turn

'We tend to think that the Butes made a fortune from their Cardiff docks,' Dr David Jenkins, the historian, said, 'but in fact they made their money from the royalties they raised on coal and land they owned in the valleys. The trouble was that marine technology kept improving, from sailing ships to steamships. When the first dock was opened in Cardiff in 1839 the typical merchant vessel was a sailing ship of two or three hundred tons. By 1900 the typical ship was a tramp steamer loading five thousand tons. As vessels grew larger the docks quickly became outdated and the company had to build more docks to keep up with the growing capacity of ships.'

Indeed, congestion in the docks and on the coal railways from the valleys became an acute problem. In the 1870s Rhondda coal tycoons grew increasingly concerned over the traffic jams in the docks and furious at the heavy charges demanded by the Marquess of Bute. The most prominent owner, David Davies of Llandinam, and his ally John Cory,

STILL SUPPLYING STEAM!

THE WORLD: "'Tis little Wales that keeps me spinning!"

decided to bypass Cardiff by building new docks at Barry fed by a fifteen-mile railway from the Rhondda. They fought the opposition of the Bute faction, which did not want to lose its monopoly, and opened the dock in 1889. You might say that Barry was built on anger.

In any case it played its part in phenomenal growth and before the end of its first year exported a million tons of coal. South Wales was a global energy capital, its outpouring almost volcanic, and the Bristol Channel a world artery. A cartoon of 1909 showed 'Dame Wales' delivering a lump of steam coal to the world, with the world exclaiming: ''Tis little Wales that keeps me spinning.' Cardiff was the potent and powerful commercial centre where the brokers, shipowners and the Coal Exchange ran the coal trade. Cardiff did not build ships - it repaired them. By 1913 there were sixteen repair companies.

In that year the south Wales coal industry was at its zenith. A fifth of the coal moving in the world was Welsh. Barry overhauled Cardiff and became the champion coal exporter of the world, shipping out eleven million tons to Cardiff's ten million. In one day in 1913 there were thirty-eight ships loading coal at Barry, chiefly for South America and the railways of Argentina. The coal trade forged close connections between Wales and Argentina.

A coal train arrived in Barry from the Rhondda every fifteen minutes. The wagons had doors at only one end so that they had to be marshalled correctly and run out to the dock edge to tip their loads. As the coal was tipped into a ship's hold brawny trimmers used huge shovels to spread it evenly to ensure the ship's stability, a job perhaps worse than mining. Everything was smothered in coal dust. It lay in a thick sheen on the water.

After the tumult, quiet days in Barry

Tough guys: coal trimmers in south Wales

Spiritual home from home: the Norwegian church in Cardiff docks

Railways and ships: motif on the Pierhead Building, Cardiff Bay

Ships from south Wales delivered coal to naval bunkers and railway companies all over the world. Many of those which served the Mediterranean headed for the Black Sea after discharging their coal. There they loaded Ukrainian cereals for Germany and Belgium and came back to Wales for more coal. Many of the ships on the Argentina run returned with grain for Europe.

Out of the energy, growth and wealth of south Wales grew a vigorous and diverse society. In Cardiff's docklands a distinctive multiracial community, African, Indian and Arab, developed from the 1860s. The Norwegian church in the docks, the first seamen's mission outside Norway, is a reminder of the strong links with Scandinavia and the thriving trade in pine pit props. The author Roald Dahl was born in Llandaff, the son of a Norwegian shipbroker.

'There was an incredible mixture of people in the docks, from the poorest seamen to the millionaires. Bute Street ruled the world,' said David Jenkins. 'The turning point was the First World War. The Treaty of Versailles, which brought the war formally to an end, was signed by David Lloyd George, the Prime

Only the ghosts of ships: a dock in Cardiff Bay

Minister. It required Germany to make reparations, partly in coal, which undermined the Welsh coal industry.

'At that time oil was an increasingly important fuel and no major coal-fired warships were built after 1914. It was not until 1957 that oil overtook coal as the world's main provider of energy, but the decline had started in Wales in the 1920s.'

Just as the port of Cardiff had risen, so it fell. For many years there was dereliction in the docklands on a vast scale and Cardiff did not seem to know what to do with it. Today, in the throes of renewal, it is Cardiff Bay, a place of architectural adventure, cultural controversy, a work in progress. There were a hundred and twenty shipowners in Cardiff during its heyday, David Jenkins said. Today there are two. 'They've obviously had to adapt to the present age, but there are still Cardiff ships at sea and the docks remain active.'

At the heart of Cardiff Bay's development is the barrage, the huge dam. 'I can't help feeling that it is almost a metaphor for the decline of Cardiff as a port. We see it holding back the sea, the sea which washed into the city centre for centuries and was Cardiff's life blood.'

Barry had a renaissance with the Geest banana boats, but they withdrew in 1993 and today the docks are very quiet. 'Its commercial future,' David Jenkins said, 'is perhaps not in shipping but in the development of land, with the water a feature around which you build pleasant housing.'

Milford Haven, a symbol of oil's significance, deals mostly in oil imports and is the fifth largest cargo port in Britain and the busiest in Wales. At the eastern end of the Bristol Channel, Newport also thrives, handling timber, steel and coal. Like any docks it is a tough man's world but, perhaps as evidence of the way things change, its operations have been run for three years by the notably determined and personable Emma Lewis, aged thirty-two. I talked to her as we watched cranes unload telegraph poles from a ship and asked what it was like managing a famously rugged group of dockers.

Still bustling: Newport Docks

'I started my career with Associated British Ports ten years ago, shovelling coal and piling up bananas and driving fork lift trucks with these men. I went away and worked in other ports, Swansea and Port Talbot, and now I've returned as their manager. I have a lot of respect for them and the work they do and they wouldn't want my job. So it works well, with mutual respect. It helps a lot that I started at the bottom, getting my hands dirty. I have a rude nickname, just as they have. I've done the job and I empathize with them and try not to be unreasonable. I'm here with them a lot of the time, if not all of the time.

'I graduated with a degree in mechanical engineering, looked for a job and found this, the cutting edge, out in all winds and weathers, dealing with the ships, the captains, the international trade, the cargoes, the foreign languages, and the hours that go with all of that. Newport is thriving. There really is excitement in being here.'

Many seaports in Wales were strongly associated with a particular product. Much of the bustle in Caernarfon from the

In the heyday of slate, schooners crowd to load cargoes at Caernarfon Quay

Sofas, tables and chairs: Customs tariffs posted at New Quay emphasise the importance of the coastal trade in the years before good roads and railways

middle of the nineteenth century revolved around the slate that came down from the quarries of the Nantlle Valley. The quays beside the castle, now a car park, were for many years covered with stacks of slate ready for loading onto schooners. When the quays were full, ships waited their turn outside the harbour. The cargoes ranged from sixty to a hundred and fifty tons and most were sailed to Liverpool and Runcorn and trans-shipped to roof houses in the Midlands.

Others took slate to Dublin and across the Atlantic.

Shipowners put planks on top of the slate cargo and migrants on top of the planks. For thirty years there was a regular trade between Caernarfon, Boston, Quebec and New York. The ships unloaded slate and hopeful fortune-seekers and loaded timber that was often used in the building of new schooners.

Owners and captains were hunters of sorts, always on the lookout for a cargo. It remains the story today, the ports grappling with the economic fortunes that flow and ebb like the tide, knowing that they must evolve, adapt or wither away.

A SHIP HAS BEEN SIGHTED
in this quarter
ENGAGING IN THE UNLAWFUL ACT OF

SMUGGLING

whosoever can lay information
leading to the capture of this ship
or its crew

will receive a reward of

£500

From His Majesty's Government

This 19th day of October 1782

5. Five and Twenty Ponies

Smuggling is as old as tax. In any story of the sea you soon meet the smugglers. In what we might call the storybook era of smuggling, from the end of the seventeenth century into the nineteenth, the coast of Wales, with its numerous coves, was perfect for clandestine deliveries of tobacco, lace, tea, brandy and much else.

There was big money involved and the smugglers ran professional and businesslike operations. They favoured places like Brandy Cove, on the south coast of Gower, where concealing woodland extended to the sandy beach. They chose moonless nights and sailed their ships as close to the beach as they could. A well-organized shore party waited among the rocks, keeping a sharp look-out for Customs officers. Brief lantern signals were exchanged and, as quietly as they could, the smugglers lowered their cargoes into boats.

The men on the beach swiftly loaded boxes and barrels onto broad shoulders and the backs of horses and ponies. In minutes the goods were being dispersed through the countryside. The Customs estimated that at least five thousand barrels of brandy were landed on the Gower coast in a six month period of 1795. A path near Bishopston is still known as Smugglers' Lane and evokes the excitement of the men who worked the illicit night shift and cached their goods in caves, cellars and barns. Farmers and others were drawn into the trade as suppliers of horses and owners of hiding places. Almost everyone seemed to

A gleam of light at Brandy Cove: a signalling lantern

be involved. Smugglers outfoxed the Customs by stowing barrels of brandy in the altar of Port Eynon church, no doubt with the connivance of the parish priest.

In 'A Smuggler's Song', Rudyard Kipling summed up the idea that there was widespread participation in the smuggling game:

> Five and twenty ponies,
> Trotting through the dark –
> Brandy for the Parson,
> 'Baccy for the Clerk.

In the nature of things, smugglers were often greedy and violent. Yet, for many years, public opinion generally favoured them. History has cast them as roguish folk heroes. It is easy to understand why. Governments needed revenue, especially to wage war or to pay off the debts incurred by war, and imposed a wide range of duties which to the popular mind were both

" FOR OUR PARSON."

onerous and unjust. For a time there was a tax on bricks and windows; and for eleven years from 1695 the authorities charged a levy on bachelors over the age of twenty-five. Clearly, being single was considered a luxury.

Smugglers are invariably associated with brandy and tobacco. They also traded in tea and heavily-taxed luxuries like silk and lace. The temptations were irresistible. In the 1790s smugglers could buy a four-gallon barrel of brandy in France for a pound and fill their pockets by selling it in Britain. A pound of tea cost seven pence in Holland, but in Britain it was nine times as much. So the smugglers had a ready market.

To their immense profit they also smuggled more mundane goods. Salt was one of them. It was vital for preserving meat during the winter, for pickling fish and curing hides. The duty charged on it hit ordinary people hard and was seen almost as a tax on survival. The smugglers brought large quantities of salt from Ireland and sold it in Wales and England for half the duty-paid price.

Many people, too, thought tobacco a necessary solace, not a luxury, and hated the heavy duty on it. It was one thing to tax silk and brandy; quite another to impose duty on such basics as soap and salt. Thus the squire in the big house found common cause with the poor in the village and on the farm: they were united in their resentment. The Customs collector at Milford Haven wrote ruefully in 1576 that 'I am so hated that I cannot execute my office for fear of danger.'

In 1804 Customs officers in Gower who seized more than four hundred casks of brandy were surrounded by angry people and forced to hand over sixteen barrels to placate them. In the following year Customs men arrived in force during a big landing of brandy at Rhossili and after a bitter brawl the smugglers fled, leaving kegs scattered on the sands. Customs officers who pounced on smugglers landing a salt cargo at New Quay in Ceredigion were violently resisted and some were badly injured in the fighting on the beach.

Twm Elias, who has made a study of smuggling, told me about two French ships which sailed into Pwllheli in 1783. Two Customs officers went aboard and were seized by the crew, tied up and confined in the hold. They heard everything that happened next. The smugglers unloaded the cargoes which were

set out on the quayside and sold off as if the whole event was a country fair. The imprisoned Customs men heard the sound of horses and carts carrying off the goods and no doubt reflected that an event so public must have had the support of the local gentry. The cargoes were sold for £16,000, a fortune in those days. The smugglers released their Customs prisoners and sailed away.

'The huge sums to be made from smuggling attracted ruthless crime syndicates,' Twm said. 'In the early nineteenth century the scale of tea smuggling was so great that about half the possible revenue from tea was not collected.'

In the 1780s a Parliamentary committee reached the conclusion that the only way to prevent smuggling was to reduce the duties charged on so many goods. But half a century passed before free trade between nations became an acceptable political idea and the government reduced the number of dutiable goods. In the meantime there was war between the smugglers and the Excise men.

In the years when so many people winked at smuggling it

was not surprising that the inhabitants of coastal villages looked on the cargoes of wrecked ships as the bounty of the seas. Ships were the chief form of transport and there were many wrecks. Stories abound of vessels driven ashore and stripped of their valuable cargoes in a few hours. In Oxwich Bay in Gower the private armies of two squires fought over the loot that spilled from a French ship blown ashore.

The Ceredigion coast, too, was notorious for its smuggling and wreck-robbing. Geraint Jenkins told me of a French ship wrecked at Penbryn in 1816. 'The local people took its cargo of wine and brandy. In the aftermath, several of my ancestors drank immoderately and died of alcohol poisoning. The Bishop of Saint David's wrote a letter to every vicar on the coast telling them to preach sermons on temperance.'

One of the by-products of the unending contest between smugglers and the excise authorities was an improvement in sailing ship performance and technology. It was in the smugglers' interests to own fast ships and to sail them hard to outstrip the pursuing Customs officers. In response, the government developed the famous single-masted revenue cutters, designed for speed, and armed them with ten nine-pounder guns with extended barrels to increase their range.

It was a backhanded compliment that in the days when the press gangs roamed ports looking for men to man the ships of the Royal Navy, the recruiting officers always rejected thieves, who were detested by sailors, but always accepted smugglers because they were outstanding seamen.

In the 1820s and 1830s revenue cutters, naval patrols and the new coastguard service gave the authorities the upper hand over smugglers in the Bristol Channel. The golden age of the brandy runners was over.

But smugglers have adapted and worked to the changing market; and there has always been a battle of wits, a contest, smugglers trying to stay ahead, the Customs hard on their heels. Modern smugglers are a long way from the popular rogues of the brandy, baccy and salt era. They trade in drugs, firearms and illegal migrants. For an insight into the problems confronting the authorities today I went out on Milford Haven aboard a patrol boat operated by the Dyfed Powys Police Marine Unit. Established in 1999, it is the only one in Wales. Its powerful inflatables, one capable of thirty knots, the other of forty, are at sea every day, covering a coastline of nearly three hundred and ninety miles from the Loughor estuary in the east up to Aberdyfi in the north.

'Many people see the west coast of Wales as a back door,' said Detective-Sergeant Nick O'Brien, 'and our job is to guard it as best we can. There's a long history of smuggling here. We are on the lookout for criminals trying to bring in drugs and guns; and we are also concerned with the threat of terrorism. Apart from that, the coast is popular with tourists and they are as entitled to a police service as much as anyone else.'

Sea cop: Detective-Sergeant Nick O'Brien of the Dyfed Powys Marine Unit

Dyfed Powys police officers in a high-speed inflatable, or 'rib', check incoming ships and yachts in Milford Haven

During our patrol, police officers boarded an incoming yacht and a ship. 'Under the Terrorism Act we have authority to ask people where they have come from, where they are going and to verify their identity. We check to see that their activities are legitimate. We speak to the master of a ship, ask for a crew list, ensuring that we know who's coming into the country. Most of the time we deal with law-abiding people and it is very rare that anyone takes exception to our asking questions. But sometimes a policeman's instinct tells you that you need to take a closer look, and so we do.'

Nick O'Brien was part of the police and Customs team that trapped a gang of smugglers on the Pembrokeshire coast in 1986. For several weeks they tracked a consignment of one and a half tons of cannabis, worth about £4 million, brought from Morocco in a fishing boat. The unloading of the booty into dinghies at the remote beach of Aberbach was just like an eighteenth-century scene.

'They were landing on the beach,' said Nick O'Brien, 'and we were hiding in the bushes, waiting for them.'

In the sixteenth and seventeenth centuries piracy was rife along the Welsh coast, especially in the Bristol Channel, and no ship was safe from the seagoing highwaymen. Pirates sallied out to plunder merchant vessels and returned to port to display and sell the goods they had stolen. There was nothing covert about it. Some men controlled fleets of pirate ships. And when Britain went to war they happily assumed the status of privateers, licensed to loot enemy ships.

Pirates operated wherever ships sailed, most notoriously in the Caribbean where the chief targets were the Spaniards whose ships were often laden with treasure and were regarded as fair game. Some pirates called themselves buccaneers, a French description of men who barbecued their meat on the beach. The Welsh buccaneer Henry Morgan made so much money from his raiding in the West Indies that he became respectable. He captured Panama in 1671, was knighted and made deputy governor of Jamaica.

Fiercer and very much more of a pirate was Bartholomew Roberts, born in 1682 in Pembrokeshire, and known as Barti Ddu, or Black Bart, the greatest predator of the seas. 'He was an honest seafarer for twenty years,' said Tom Bennett, who has studied his life, 'until he was captured by pirates on the African coast and offered the choice of death or of joining the crew. He soon became captain, an excellent leader, and caused terror on the north Atlantic.

'He had strict rules – no drink, women or boys were allowed on his ships – and he made every man swear on the Bible that he would behave. He himself was a tea drinker, well-dressed, with a liking for crimson waistcoats and breeches, and wore a huge red feather in his cocked hat. In under four years he plundered four hundred ships and amassed the equivalent in today's money of between £50 and £80 million.'

Pirate king: Bartholomew Roberts plundered scores of ships on both sides of the Atlantic until hunted down by Captain Chaloner Ogle

Roberts was such a menace to shipping in the Caribbean and along the west coast of Africa that the Royal Navy set out to hunt him down. In February 1722, after a long search, Captain Chaloner Ogle, aboard HMS *Swallow*, found Roberts's ship, *Royal Fortune*, off the African coast. He opened fire and the pirate king fell dead, slumped over a gun. His men threw him over the side, in all his finery, just as he had requested. They themselves were soon seized and tried. Fifty-two of them were hanged. Captain Ogle was knighted for ridding the Atlantic of a scourge. He, too, was a Pembrokeshire man.

6. Speed for Sale

Our nineteenth-century forebears were dazzled by speed. They believed that fast travel was a definition of progress and were excited by the record-breaking ocean passages achieved by new kinds of sailing ships and by the stagecoaches which ran to strict timetables on reliable roads. The advent of the steam engine, powering trains and ships, ushered in a new age of velocity. People began to fancy that with such machines they could conquer time itself.

The young Queen Victoria was a symbol of the exhilarating times. When she was born in 1819 the roads of Britain were ruled by the stagecoaches. Packed with mail and passengers they criss-crossed Britain at what seemed like remarkable speeds on the highways laid down by Thomas Telford and John McAdam.

When Telford constructed his masterpiece, the Menai Bridge, in 1826 the stagecoach journey from London to Holyhead was reduced to twenty-seven hours. With luck and good weather passengers could complete their journey, from Holyhead to Dublin, in half a day. Contemporary accounts are full of astonishment at such rapid travel. When the eighteen-year-old Victoria came to the throne in 1837 the steam age was getting into its stride. Railway-building was turning into a fever and the early steamships were clanking their way around the coasts in swirling plumes of gritty smoke.

The engineer Isambard Kingdom Brunel started building

The Menai Bridge, forerunner of all suspension bridges, shortened the journey from London to Dublin

the Great Western Railway from Paddington to Bristol in 1833. Five years later his wooden paddle steamship *Great Western* set off on her maiden Atlantic voyage from Bristol and reached New York in fifteen days. Great crowds flocked to see a vessel that only two weeks earlier had been on the other side of the ocean. A newspaper declared that time itself had been defeated. The *Great Western*'s voyage showed doubters that a steamship would carry enough coal to fuel a long voyage and opened the way to the epoch of the transatlantic liners.

Brunel bestrode the new age of steam and the exciting new material, iron. He thought big. Almost everything he designed was on the grand scale. He believed there was nothing he could not do and rode the tide of his confidence and genius as a railway engineer, bridge builder and creator of steamships. At Bristol in 1843 he launched his revolutionary *Great Britain*, the first large iron ship, twice the size of anything else afloat. Her powerful engine turned a propeller, rather than paddles, a truly significant advance in marine engineering, and gave her speed of twelve knots. One of those aboard her on her sea trials was Thomas

Lloyd, a Welshman, one of the brains behind maritime steam power, who would become chief engineer in the Royal Navy.

Brunel saw the *Great Britain* as his bridge into the future, the central component of his dream of joining London to New York by fast Great Western Railway train and fast ship. It was not to be. The *Great Britain* made a successful maiden voyage from Liverpool to New York in 1845 but ran aground in Ireland in 1846 and effectively ended her steamship days. She was salvaged and fitted out as a sailing vessel and spent twenty-three years carrying passengers to Australia. In the 1880s she became a storage hulk in the Falkland Islands. There she lay, forgotten, until 1970 when she was rescued, towed to Bristol and restored to her old appearance in the very dock in which Brunel built her.

In the 1840s, pursuing his vision of an Atlantic link, Brunel looked westward to Wales and extended his railway to Milford Haven, building a terminus at Neyland. Indeed this was the foundation of the town. But powerful Liverpool established itself as the chief Atlantic port. The Haven was, however, afforded a glimpse of a glory that might have been. In London in 1858 Brunel launched his third ship, the *Great Eastern*, far in advance of her time and, at more than eighteen thousand tons, twice the size of the *Great Britain*. The stresses of building her hastened her designer's end and he died in 1859.

In 1860, the *Great Eastern* called at Neyland for repairs to her screw propulsion and when the job was done thousands turned out to wave her off. A rope trailing from a spectator boat tangled with the propeller. The boat was smashed, two people drowned and, with its engine stopped, the mighty ship drifted on the tide and hit a sailing vessel before she got on her way. She was not a success as a passenger ship but because of her strength and capacity turned out to be the ideal vessel for laying the transatlantic telegraph cable.

Like Neyland, Fishguard once had its Atlantic dreams, but settled for a ferry service to Ireland. The road from London to

Water power: the Stena high speed ferry loads passengers and vehicles at Holyhead

Holyhead is an ancient and strategic one and Holyhead has always owed its importance to its proximity to Dublin. The traffic of its famous sailing packets, the mail ships that carried goods and passengers, increased considerably after the Union with Ireland in 1800. A steam packet service from Holyhead started in 1821, but the reliable sailing packets operated for many years.

The greatest of the sailing packet captains was the dashing John MacGregor Skinner. Service in the Royal Navy had left him with one arm, but that did not stop him being a daring horseman and master of the Anglesey hunt. He ate his meals with an ingenious all-in-one knife and fork, like the cutlery made for Lord Nelson. He was a captain for thirty-three years, but in 1832 a rogue wave swept him from his ship a mile off Holyhead and he drowned. To mark their esteem Holyhead's people raised a memorial pillar, Skinner's Monument. It rises on a hill overlooking the harbour and its one and a half mile breakwater, the longest in Britain.

How Brunel would marvel at the fast and spacious modern ships that link Holyhead to Dublin. The high-speed ferry, introduced in 1993, reaches forty knots and has halved the journey time to less than two hours. Captain Tudor Roberts told me about its revolutionary type of propulsion, water jets powered by gas turbines the size of jumbo jet engines, sending a hundred tons of water through the jets in one second.

Captain Roberts was one of the team sent to Tasmania to take delivery of the first Stena high-speed ferry. It was a secret mission: the team did not know exactly what kind of vessel they would be collecting. The voyage home to Holyhead, by way of Singapore, Sri Lanka and the Suez Canal, took them three weeks.

'The excitement of handling the craft never palls,' Tudor Roberts said. 'On every trip the sea conditions and weather are different. And so are the passengers.'

The *Stena Adventurer*, brought into service in 2003, carries fifteen hundred people and three miles of cars. On its vast bridge, packed with computers, I talked with Captain Alec Robertson, a retired Holyhead ferry captain.

Stena Adventurer, newest addition to the fleet, at berthing trials in Holyhead

'I first went to sea at fifteen in 1933, on a ship carrying coal from south Wales to Montreal. The next voyage was to the River Plate and the next to Queensland. I didn't think it an adventurous life: I was busy obeying commands and for me it was a hard life. In 1939 I was on watch in the Atlantic and the captain, who was listening to the wireless, told me to go to his safe and take out an envelope. I brought it to him and he opened it and said war had broken out between Germany and Britain.

'For three years I was on the Atlantic convoys. I remember a night when we were off Cape Wrath in Scotland, bound from Halifax to London, and I suddenly saw a white flash, then a red flash. A ship had been torpedoed and she went down in nineteen seconds with all hands. The convoy scattered. Another time we were attacked by two aircraft. I saw the pilot, saw the bomb coming towards us. Bloody hell, I said, I'm dead. But he missed us, from that height, almost unbelievable.

'We got to London and saw the big raids of September 1940, when everything in the docks was hit. We were kicking incendiary bombs off the deck. I did more trips across the Atlantic and then started in Holyhead on the ferries in 1941 and eventually became a captain.'

A ship at sea can never be a democracy. There is room for only one commanding figure, he who must be obeyed, the bearer of responsibility for the ship and the lives of passengers. There is a complex mix of experience, seamanship, navigation and instinct. The captain must be manager of people, the maker of morale. Many men are excellent sailors but only a few have that certain extra talent that makes a ship's master, the elusive quality of command.

'It's a pressure job and requires a special aptitude,' Captain Robertson said. 'Calmness and knowledge make a captain, a temperament not many people possess. I've known top class seamen who couldn't be captains because they lacked that vital temperament.

'As we can see on this modern bridge, ships have all sorts of electronic equipment and navigational aids. But the sea is still the sea and managing a ship demands constant vigilance. When you have two thousand passengers on board you dwell on it. It's pretty frightening. You can never relax: you have ships crossing your path, overtaking you, ships without lights, little boats fishing without lights, all the problems of coming into port.

'My own experience was that in those large numbers of ferry passengers you sometimes had sick and dying people and sometimes a baby born on board. One night a couple begged me to marry them. I told them I couldn't, that it was not true that captains could marry people. Well, said the man, can't you say just a few words – to tide us over the weekend?'

One evening I joined Captain George Gunn for a cruise aboard the *Balmoral*, once part of the fleet of Campbell White Funnel ships. Campbell steamers were familiar on the coasts of Wales and carried passengers up and down the Bristol Channel and on the north coast for almost a century.

Veteran: the *Balmoral*, once a familiar sight in the Bristol Channel as part of the Campbell fleet, still cruises the Thames

George Gunn had a distinguished seagoing career. He joined his first ship in his native Scotland as an apprentice of seventeen in 1941; and by that time more than a thousand British merchant vessels had been sunk by enemy action. He made his first convoy voyage to West Africa, then to Cape Town, Aden, Port Said and on to Haifa, to deliver urgently-needed supplies to British forces fighting in north Africa. His ship then sailed for Bombay and back to Cape Town and Britain.

'It was an exciting and rewarding way to grow up,' he reflected. His next voyage took him in convoy across the Atlantic to New York, then to Cape Town, the Gulf, India, Australia, around Cape Horn to the Caribbean and back across the Atlantic. Later he had the harrowing experience of being in a convoy mauled by submarines and dive-bombers, but somehow his ship survived to bring much-needed copper ore to Britain.

In 1948 he joined the Campbell steamer company and began his long affair with the romantic paddle steamers of the Bristol Channel. After the deep-sea years of the war, and the long absences from home, one attraction of working with Campbells was the prospect of enjoying a proper family life. Many people in Wales remember their holiday trips in such ships as the *Cardiff Queen, Bristol Queen, Empress Queen, Ravenswood, Glen Gower, Glen Usk* and *Britannia*. They linked Cardiff, Penarth, Barry, Porthcawl, Mumbles and Tenby, Bristol, Minehead, Ilfracombe, Lundy and many other places. Along the north Wales coast they worked Holyhead, Caernarfon, Menai Bridge, Llandudno and Liverpool.

In a varied career, George Gunn worked as a Swansea pilot and a master of Bristol Channel pilot ships, guiding more than three thousand vessels in an out of port. He was also superintendent of Townsend Ferries at Dover and worked in Greece and in Canada.

On the bridge of the *Balmoral* we talked about the old Campbell fleet and particularly about the paddle steamers.

'What the paddle ships had in common was that none of them was easy to handle. They all presented real challenges to a seaman, especially in the conditions of the Bristol Channel where you have huge tides and strong south-westerly winds. Being the master of a paddle steamer there was a very specialized job. I worked in many places, but I never came across anything like the Bristol Channel.'

Acknowledgements

My thanks to Captain Gwyn Pari Huws, former Marine Superintendent, Liverpool; Tom Cunliffe, author and seaman; Dr Bill Jones, School of History and Archaeology, Cardiff University; Dr David Jenkins, Senior Curator Maritime and Transport, National Museum and Gallery of Wales; Dr Geraint Jenkins, former Curator Welsh Folk Museum; Val Howells, author and seaman; Owain T.P. Roberts, nautical archaeologist; Captain Alec Robertson, Holyhead; Captain Tudor Roberts, Holyhead; Emma Lewis, Newport Docks; Dr Alan Scarth, Merseyside Maritime Museum; Twm Elias, senior lecturer, Plas Tan y Bwlch; Tom Bennett, writer; Ifan Jones, Hon. Secretary, Moelfre Lifeboat, Anglesey; Anthony Barclay, Coxswain Moelfre Lifeboat; Chris Williams, retired lighthouse keeper; Susan Wilkinson, Toronto; Richard Burnell, Holyhead Maritime Museum; the late Captain George Gunn; David James, West Wales Maritime Heritage Society; Rob Scourfield, Pembrokeshire Coast National Park Authority; Detective-Sergeant Nick O'Brien, Dyfed Powys Police; Bryan Hope, Amlwch Heritage Centre.

Trevor Fishlock

Illustration Acknowledgements

The publisher thanks the following for the illustrations, John Briggs: pp. 13, 61, 64b; Ceredigion Museum: 39; Tom Cunliffe: 26, 27; Trevor Fishlock: 29, 53, 54, 79, 80; Gwynedd Archive Service: 47, 68, 86; O.T.P. Roberts 48; Library of Congress 37; William Linnard: 46; Geoff Lloyd: 8, 22, 24, 32, 33, 35, 40, 42, 44, 52, 57, 59, 67, 91; Mervyn Matthews: 64t; Moelfre Lifeboat Station: 25; National Maritime Museum: 82b; Seren: 11, 14, 15, 16, 18, 20, 21, 28, 43, 50, 51, 55, 56, 63, 65, 66, 69, 71, 77, 84, 93